The Federal Gift Tax:
History, Law, and Economics

by

David Joulfaian
US Department of the Treasury

OTA Paper 100   **November 2007**

OTA Papers is an occasional series of reports on the research, models, and datasets developed to inform and improve Treasury's tax policy analysis. The papers are works in progress and subject to revision. Views and opinions expressed are those of the authors and do not necessarily represent official Treasury positions or policy. OTA Papers are distributed in order to document OTA analytic methods and data and invite discussion and suggestions for revision and improvement. Comments are welcome and should be directed to the authors.

Office of Tax Analysis
US Department of the Treasury
1500 Pennsylvania Avenue, NW
Washington, DC 20220

The paper benefited from comments by Robert Carroll, Donald Kiefer, and Michael Udell. The invaluable research assistance of Margaret Rolley is gratefully acknowledged. Comments and corrections are welcome to david.joulfaian@do.treas.gov.

Abstract

The gift tax was first enacted in 1924, repealed in 1926, overhauled and reintroduced in 1932. At its peak in fiscal year 1999, it raised $4.6 billion in revenues, before the recent phased-in tax rate reductions ushered by the Economic Growth and Tax Relief Reconciliation Act of 2001 (EGTRRA) took effect. It is noteworthy that the gift tax was first enacted as a protective measure to minimize estate and income tax avoidance, and not for its direct revenue yield. Similarly, EGTRRA, while phasing out the estate tax, retained the gift tax for the very same reasons.

Unlike the estate tax which faces an uncertain future, the gift tax is little affected by recent legislative proposals and will remain part of the tax code for the foreseeable future. Nevertheless, the gift tax has been the subject of little scrutiny and studies of its economic implications are rare. This paper is an attempt to fill this void. It traces the evolution of the gift tax since its inception, and sketches out the structure of the tax and its complex interactions with the income and estate taxes.

The paper also provides an overview of the direct fiscal contribution of the gift tax, and traces the number of taxpayers over time as well as their attributes. It concludes with a discussion of the behavioral effects of the gift tax and a review of the scant literature. These include empirical evidence on the choice between gifts and bequests, timing of gifts, and compliance among others.

TABLE OF CONTENTS

TABLES

FIGURES

I. INTRODUCTION

The gift tax is likely to remain a permanent feature of the federal tax code in sharp contrast to the estate tax which faces an uncertain future. Indeed, legislation enacted in 2001, specifically the Economic Growth and Tax Relief Reconciliation Act of 2001 (EGTRRA), and more recent proposals have called for the repeal or dramatic scale back of the estate tax, while leaving much of the gift tax unaffected.

The gift tax was first enacted in 1924, repealed in 1926, overhauled and reintroduced in 1932. It raised $1.9 billion in tax revenues in fiscal year 2006, down from a peak of $4.6 billion in revenues it raised in fiscal year 1999, before the recent phased-in tax rate reductions. It is noteworthy that the gift tax was not enacted for its direct revenue yield. Rather it was introduced as a protective measure to minimize estate and income tax avoidance.[1] Similarly, EGTRRA, while phasing out the estate tax, retained the gift tax for the very same reason.

During the congressional deliberations in 1932 leading to the enactment of the gift tax, one individual is reported to have made about $100 million in gifts; another to have made gifts of about $50 million (Roosevelt, 1938: 313-14). Considering that the entire yield of the estate tax in 1932 was $400 million, the tax-free inter-vivos transfers of $150 million by these two individuals alone, not to mention likely gifts by scores of others, are

---

[1] The stated purpose of the proposed introduction of the gift tax in the House Committee report was "To assist in the collection of the income and estate taxes and prevent their avoidance through the splitting of estates during the lifetime of a taxpayer." See House of Representatives (1932, pp. 8).

indicative of the potency of the gift tax.[2] Yet, to date, the gift tax has been the subject of little scrutiny and studies of its economic implications are rare.

The purpose of this paper is to fill the void in the literature, and shed light on the inner workings of the gift tax and its behavioral implications. More specifically, it traces the evolution of the gift tax, describes its structure, and explores some of its economic consequences. Section II traces developments in the federal gift tax since its inception. Section III describes the current structure of the gif tax, focusing on the tax base and rate schedule, as well as how the tax is administered. It also explains how the gift tax interacts with estate and income taxes, and concludes with a mathematical presentation of the various complex features of the tax.

Section IV examines the fiscal contribution of the gift tax, and in particular the revenue collected by the federal government. Section V focuses on the taxpayers, i.e., the donors, and provides information on their attributes. Section VI explores the behavioral effects of the gift tax, and summarizes the empirical findings in the literature.

A concluding comment is provided in Section VII which address the failures of the gift tax in meetings its objectives. A number of valuation practices undermine the efficacy of the gift tax. In addition, and despite its role as a protective tax, there is little harmonization between the gift tax, the estate tax, and the income tax.

---

[2] Equally impressive is the acceleration in gifts that took place in 1934, 1935, and 1976 prior to the introduction of higher gift tax rates.

II.   HISTORY OF THE FEDERAL GIFT TAX

A number of taxes were increased in 1932 to bolster the Depression era finances of the Treasury. On June 6, 1932, the maximum estate tax rate was increased from 20 to 45 percent. As part of the same enabling legislation, the current gift tax was introduced to shore up revenues by preempting estate and income tax avoidance. The tax evolved during the next seven decades, as illustrated in Table 1.

At the time of its introduction, the tax rate schedule was set at 75 percent of the rates prevailing under the estate tax. As noted in Harriss (1940, p. 147), the gift tax rate was deliberately set below that of the estate tax so as to create incentives for the wealthy to accelerate their transfers as well as the ensuing tax liability to the cash starved Treasury. The benefit to the wealthy from such acceleration is that paying the gift tax would be equivalent to pre-paying the estate tax, but at a significant discount. The more immediate benefit is that gifts likely to have been made in the future are now made during a regime of lower tax rates.

The gift tax was enacted in 1932 with a tax rate schedule that ranged from 0.75 to 33.75 percent (see Table 2). The tax provided an annual exclusion of $5,000 per recipient. This was coupled with an additional exemption of $50,000 applied to cumulated lifetime taxable gifts, as reported in Table 3. In other words, transfers in a given year are taxable if they exceed the annual exclusion and when cumulative lifetime taxable gifts exceed $50,000.

3

On May 11, 1934, the maximum estate tax rate was increased to 60 percent, and the gift tax rate to 45 percent. The legislated gift tax increase, however, was made effective on January 1, 1935, some seven months after the enactment date. On August 31, 1935, estate and gift tax rates were raised to 70 and 52.50 percent, respectively. The lifetime gift tax exemption was reduced to $40,000. Once again, the change in the gift tax was made effective the beginning of the following year for a delay of four months.

On June 25, 1940, a surtax of 10 percent on estate and gift taxes was introduced. This had the effect of increasing the maximum gift tax rate from 52.50 to 57.75 percent. These increases were temporary in nature and set to expire at the end of 1945. Unlike earlier legislation, the enacted increases went into effect almost immediately. Legislation enacted in September 1941 further raised rates except in the case of transfers in excess of $50 million, with maximum estate and gift tax rates set at 77 and 57.75 percent, respectively. It also reduced the annual exclusion to $3,000 and the lifetime exemption to $30,000. Not surprisingly, gift tax increases once again did not take effect until the beginning of the following calendar year.

The Revenue Act of 1948 introduced the marital deduction for spousal transfers, and limited it to 50 percent of lifetime gifts. Prior to this Act, spousal transfers were fully taxable. But under this Act, transfers of community property continued to be denied a marital deduction. The stated purpose of this change was to harmonize the treatment with community property states where the spouse shared in the value of the community property.

The Revenue Act of 1950 made gifts taking place within 3 years of death, up from two, subject to estate tax if they are made "in contemplation of death." Furthermore, and in 1975, Section 527 was added to the Internal Revenue Code (P.L. 93-635) to clarify the tax treatment of gifts to political organizations. This Act exempted from the gift tax gifts to political organizations made after May 7, 1974.[3] Otherwise, and with the exception of the introduction of the Internal Revenue Code of 1954, much of the gift tax remained unchanged through 1976.

Since its inception, the gift tax operated independently of the estate tax. While gifts made within two years (later three) from the date of death were included in the gross estate for estate tax purposes when deemed to have been made in "contemplation of death," for all practical purposes estate and gift taxes operated as two separate taxes. All of that changed with the enactment of the Tax Reform Act of 1976 (TRA76). The estate and gift tax rate schedules were unified with a maximum tax rate of 70 percent effective for transfers as of January 1, 1977. The statutory estate tax rate was thus reduced from 77 percent and applied to cumulative gifts and bequests, while it was raised from 57.75 percent in the case of gifts. Consistent with the earlier pattern, tax rate changes took effect some 3 months after the enactment date of October 4, 1976. TRA76 also replaced the $30,000 exemption with a tax credit of $30,000, scheduled to increase to $47,000, which applied to the cumulative gifts and bequests for the years 1977 through 1981. This Unified Tax Credit was equivalent to an exemption that increased in steps from $120,667 to 175,625.

---

[3] It is not clear whether the IRS would have enforced the taxation of such transfers.

TRA76 also required gifts made within 3 years of death, to be included in gross estate at death regardless of whether the gifts were made "in contemplation of death."[4]

TRA76 expanded the marital deduction. The deduction exempted the first $100,000 in spousal gifts, but kept it at 50 percent of lifetime transfers in excess of $200,000. With congressional concerns over tax avoidance schemes in the form of generation skipping trusts, TRA76 also introduced the Generation Skipping Transfer Tax (GSTT). The GSTT applied to transfers from trusts to beneficiaries, after an exemption of $250,000 per deemed donor, but did not apply to direct transfers from donors (e.g. grandparents).

The Economic Recovery Tax Act of 1981 (ERTA81) introduced the unlimited marital deduction[5] It also reduced the maximum tax rate from 70 percent to 50 percent phased in over a four-year period beginning in 1982. These changes, enacted on August 31, 1981, set the maximum rate at 65 percent in 1982, 60 percent in 1983, 55 percent in 1984, and 50 percent in later years. ERTA81 also increased the effective exemption in steps to $600,000 by 1987. Legislation enacted in 1984, however, froze the scheduled rate reduction at 55 percent for a period of three years. The rate was again frozen at 55 percent in 1987 for another five years[6], and set to 55 percent permanently in 1993.

---

[4] This change has the effect of raising the estate tax rate on gift donors. Through 1976, gifts were added to the estate but only if they were made in contemplation of death. This created significant opportunities for donors to make gifts prior to estate tax increases, as it was invariably difficult to prove motive. Beginning in 1977, as the two taxes were unified, all gifts made within three years of the date of death are added back to the estate.

[5] Recall that no marital deduction was allowed for community property before 1982. See Section 2523(f) prior to repeal by P.L. 97-34.

[6] The Omnibus Budget Reconciliation Act of 1987 (OBRA87) also phased out the benefits of graduated rates for transfers between $10,000,000 and $21,800,000, introducing a "bubble" with a marginal tax rate

ERTA81 also exempted the payments of tuition and medical expenses from gift taxation. It also expended the annual exclusion from $3,000 to $10,000. In addition, gifts made within 3 years of death, became no longer included in the gross estate. Instead, gift taxes paid on these gifts and gifts of life insurance were added to the gross estate for purposes of computing the estate tax liability.

The Tax Reform Act of 1984 (TRA84) required the treatment of certain below-market rate loans as taxable gifts. Beginning with the Tax Reform Act of 1986 (TRA86), the GSTT applied regardless of whether the transfer is made directly by the donor to a grandchild, or through a trust as provided for in TRA76. Consequently, when transfers skip a generation as in the case of a grandchild, the underlying assets become subject to the GSTT in addition to the gift tax. The GSTT was imposed retroactively to transfers made after of September 25, 1985. This change was coupled with a temporary exemption of $2 million per donee for transfers over the period October 23, 1986 through 1989. The features of the GSTT are summarized in Table 4.

The Tax Relief Act of 1997 (TRA97) expanded the annual gift tax exclusion of $10,000 and the $1,000,000 GSTT exemption by indexing them for inflation. It also expanded the unified credit in steps so as to exempt $1,000,000 in lifetime transfers by 2006. In addition, TRA97 introduced a three year statute of limitations from the date a gift tax return is filed.

---

of 60 percent (a surtax of 5 percent). Taxable gifts and estates in excess of $10 million faced a flat tax rate of 55 percent.

EGTRRA in 2001 introduced more dramatic, albeit temporary, changes. The maximum tax rate was gradually reduced to 35 percent in 2010, the "bubble" rate of 60 percent, or 5 percent surtax, was repealed effective in 2002. The lifetime exemption was increased to $1,000,000 in 2002. In addition, the GSTT is repealed in 2010. In 2011, however, the tax treatment of gifts reverts to the pre-EGTRRA law, as amended by TRA97. Table 5 provides a summary of these temporary features of transfer taxes.

III.   DESCRIPTION OF THE CURRENT GIFT TAX

The gift tax is computed annually by applying the tax rate schedule to gifts, over some threshold, cumulated over life. At death, cumulated taxable gifts are added to the taxable estate to derive the estate tax liability. The donor is generally responsible for paying the gift tax. Under special arrangements, however, the donee or recipient may agree to pay the tax instead.

1.   The Tax Base

The gift tax applies to lifetime transfers of cash, stocks, bonds, real estate, and businesses, among other assets. Real estate, regardless where it is located in the world, is included in taxable gifts. Similarly, indirect gifts, such as cancellation of indebtedness, are subject to the gift tax. [7] Assets transferred are generally valued at their market value at the date of the gift (or appraised value in the absence of a publicly tradable market).

---

[7] Section 2511

By virtue of the unlimited marital deduction, gifts to a spouse are excluded in computing taxable gifts.[8] Also excluded are amounts donated to charitable organizations and federal, state and local governments.[9] Gifts to political organizations are also not subject to tax.[10] Direct payments of medical expenses or tuition of a student are also excluded.[11] In addition, the tax Code provides for an annual exclusion of $10,000, or $20,000 in split gifts by husband and wife per donee, indexed for inflation beginning in 1998.[12]

All transfers in excess of the annual exclusion, less the various deductions and exemption, form the taxable gifts in a given year. Cumulative lifetime taxable gifts are added to the current year taxable gifts in determining the gift tax liability. The latter is offset by a unified tax credit of up to $345,800 which effectively exempts the first $1,000,000 in cumulative transfers from tax (2011 law).

Special rules apply to foreigners or nonresident aliens. If the spouse is a non US citizen, for instance, annual spousal transfers in excess of $100,000, indexed for inflation using 1997 as a base, are subject to tax.[13] Also, a gift of US property by nonresident aliens is

---

[8] Section 2523(a)

[9] Section 2522

[10] Section 2501(a)(5) as defined in Section 527(e)(1)

[11] Section 2503(e)

[12] Sections 2503(b)(1) and 2503(b)(2). The exclusion is indexed for inflation using CPI-U for the year prior to the transfer, relative to CPI-U for 1997, rounded down to the nearest $1,000. The exclusion is $12,000 for 2007.

[13] Section 2523(i)(2). The exemption is $125,000 in 2007.

taxable but do not benefit from the $1,000,000 exemption, i.e. the unified credit.[14]

However gifts of intangibles such as stocks and bonds may be exempt.[15]

2.   The Tax Rate Schedule

The tax rate schedule ranges from 18 percent on the first $10,000 to 55 percent for the excess over $3,000,000 of taxable gifts (and estates). The tax rate schedule applicable in 2011 is shown in the last column of Table 2, which applies to cumulative lifetime taxable gifts. By virtue of the unified credit which exempts the first $1 million in 2011, the lowest applicable tax rate is 41 percent; the infra marginal tax rate is zero.[16]

A unique feature of the gift tax is that it applies on a tax exclusive basis. In other words, the gift tax is based on the amount received by the donee or beneficiary and not the total amount, including tax, relinquished by the donor. To illustrate the implications of this, consider the hypothetical example where an individual facing a gift tax rate of 0.50 wishing to transfer $300 in wealth. He transfers $200 to his children in gifts and pays half of it or $100 in gift tax, for total transfers of $300. While the statutory rate is 0.50, the effective tax rate is only 0.33, or 100/300. In contrast, the tax liability would be $150 under the estate tax, or 50 percent of 300.

---

[14] Section 2505(a)

[15] Section 2501(a)(2)

3.   Generation Skipping Transfers

When transfers, either testamentary (at death) or inter-vivos during life, skip a generation, as in the case of a grandchild, the underlying assets become subject to the GSTT. This tax applies in addition to the gift tax. Transfers are taxed at the maximum estate tax rate[17], after an exemption of $1,000,000, indexed for inflation beginning in 1998.[18]

4.   Interaction with the Estate Tax

As noted earlier, and beginning in 1977, the gift tax shares a common rate schedule with the estate tax. Cumulative lifetime taxable gifts in excess of the allowable exemption are added to the taxable estate in computing the estate tax. To avoid double taxation, however, a credit is provided for previously paid gift taxes. Also, the unified credit is used up to reduce the gift tax is no longer available to offset the estate tax.

In addition, and beginning in 1982, the gift tax paid within three years of the date death is included in the gross estate and is subject to the estate tax.[19] In other words, donors lose much of the benefit of the tax exclusive nature of the gift tax when transfers are made close to the date of death.

---

[16] This unified credit and the benefit of graduated rates are phased out by applying a rate of five percent surtax on transfers between $10,000,000 and $24,100,000. In other words, the marginal tax rate is 60 percent in this "bubble" range.

[17] Section 2602.

[18] Section 2631(a).

[19] Section 2035(b).

5.   Interaction with the Income Tax

Capital gains taxation provides another critical difference in the treatment of gifts and bequests. Capital gains accrued by the donor are carried over to the recipient in the case of gifts, but stepped up at death in case of bequests. Thus, donees may become subject to capital gains taxes after the sale of assets received as gifts. To avoid double taxation and subject accrued gains to both gift and income taxes, basis is stepped up for gift taxes paid. However, basis is increased only by the gift tax pro-rated to accrued gains.[20]

6.   Administration

A.   Filing Requirements

Donors making gifts in excess of the annual exclusion of $10,000, indexed for inflation, are required to file Form 709, the Federal Gift Tax Return. This requirement is in force even though the gift tax does not apply until the unified credit is exhausted. In addition to gifts made in the current calendar year, taxpayers are also required to report cumulative gifts made in the past.

Beginning in 1982, cumulative taxable gifts and gift taxes paid are reported on the Federal estate tax return, Form 706, to aid in the determination of the estate tax liability. Taxable gifts are added to the taxable estate, and a tentative estate tax liability is computed. This is reduced by a credit for previously paid gift taxes. In addition, the gift tax paid on gifts made within three years of the date of death are reported on Schedule G,

---

[20] In other words, and assuming accrued gains share β and gift tax rate τ, taxable gains are $\beta(1-\tau) \geq 0$. Prior to 1977, basis was increased by the full amount of the gift tax, but not to exceed the selling price, with taxable gains of $(\beta-\tau) \geq 0$.

and are included in the gross estate reported on Form 706, the estate tax return. Similarly,

transfers of life insurance made within three years are also included in Schedule G.[21]

B. Due Dates

The gift tax on transfers made in a given year is due on April 15 of the following calendar

year. The gift tax return is also due on the same date, but can be extended for 6 months

by filing Form 8892. Those filing an extension to file income tax returns may instead

complete Form 4868 or 2350.

C. Statute of Limitations

Taxable gifts are typically added to the taxable estate in determining the estate tax

liability. Estates are required to attach to the estate tax return schedules documenting all

prior year gifts. Having all the combined documents available for their review, IRS

examiners often waited for the filing of the estate tax return to audit the gift tax returns

filed during life. All of that was changed with the enactment of TRA97 which introduced

a three year statute of limitations for gift tax returns filed.

7.   A Mathematical Presentation

A. The Gift Tax

A unique feature of the gift tax is that it applies on a tax exclusive basis. In other words,

for a donor with wealth W facing a statutory gift tax rate ϑ_g, the effective gift tax rate is:

---

[21] Note that the bulk of amounts reported on Schedule G of the estate tax returns are revocable trust assets and do not reflect lifetime transfers. These assets, while subject to the estate tax, by-pass probate.

(1) $\quad \dfrac{\tau_g}{1+\tau_g}$

resulting in a gift tax liability of:

(2) $\quad Tax_G = \dfrac{\tau_g}{1+\tau_g}W$

and tax price of:

(3) $\quad P_G = 1+\vartheta_g.$

i.e., at a tax rate of 0.55, a donor will give up \$1.55 for every \$1 received by the beneficiary.

When the underlying asset is stock, real estate, or some other appreciable property, then the tax implications of gifts become more complicated. Capital gains taxes may apply to gains accrued by the donor, as well as to gains accumulated by the recipient before the underlying asset is disposed of n years after receiving the gift when the donor passes away. Defining $\daleth$ as the donor's share of accrued gains in the asset, then the tax on gifts becomes:

(4) $\quad TAX_G = \left(\dfrac{\tau_g + \dfrac{\tau_c \beta \tau_g}{1-\tau_c \beta} + \dfrac{\tau_c \beta(1-\tau_g)}{(1+\delta)^n} + \dfrac{\tau_c\left[(1+\pi)^n - 1\right]}{(1+\delta)^n} + \dfrac{\rho \tau_e \tau_g}{(1+\delta)^n}}{1+\tau_g + \dfrac{\tau_c \beta \tau_g}{1-\tau_c \beta}} \right) W$

where τ_c is the capital gains tax rate, τ_e the estate tax rate, π is the asset appreciation rate, δ is the donor's discount rate, and ρ the probability of dying within three years from the date gifts were made. The first term reflects the gift tax paid by the donor. The second

14

term reflects capital gains taxes that the donor may have to pay if assets are liquidated to pay the gift tax. The third term reflects capital gains taxes expected to be paid by the beneficiary on gains accrued by the donor. Such gains, however, are reduced by gift taxes to avoid double taxation. The fourth term reflects capital gains taxes on gains accrued by the donee or recipient, where gifts received have appreciated at the rate π. The fifth term accounts for additional estate taxes on gifts made within three years of the date of death. If the donor dies within 3 years, the gift tax itself becomes taxable under the estate tax; gifts lose much of the benefit of getting taxed on a tax exclusive basis.[22] In its simplest form, the tax in equation (4) represents the sum of present taxes and the present value of future taxes.

The gift tax price becomes:

$$(5) \qquad P_G = \frac{\left(1 + \tau_g + \frac{\tau_c \beta \tau_g}{1 - \tau_c \beta}\right)(1 + \delta)^n}{(1 + \pi)^n - \tau_c \beta(1 - \tau_g) - \tau_c\left[(1 + \pi)^n - 1\right] - \rho \tau_e \tau_g}$$

Setting τ_c=0 and β=0 in (5), modifies (1) to reflect the probability of subjecting the gift tax to the estate tax.

B. The Estate Tax

In contrast, with estate tax rate τ_e the estate tax liability is:

_____

[22] See Joulfaian (2005, 2000) for an expanded discussion of the derivation. This equation can be further complicated by introducing borrowing and transferring cash as a way to avoid capital gains taxes (Auten and Joulfaian, 2001), or endogenizing portfolio allocation between cash or equivalent and appreciable assets. One may ignore all future taxes if bequests are not an alternative consideration.

$$(6) \quad TAX_E = \frac{\tau_e(1+\pi)^n W}{(1+\delta)^n}$$

where wealth W appreciates at the rate π until the death of the donor in period n, with the tax liability discounted to the present at the rate δ.

The price of bequests is:

$$(7) \quad P_B = \frac{(1-\tau_e)^{-1}(1+\delta)^n}{(1+\pi)^n}$$

or simply

$$(8) \quad P_B = \frac{1}{1-\tau_e}$$

when $\pi = \delta$ where the underlying asset appreciates at the individuals discount rate. [23] At a tax rate of 0.55, the tax price is 2.22. The parent will have to save \$2.22 for every dollar in inheritances received by the children.

C. Generation Skipping Transfers

The Tax Reform Act of 1986 introduced a generation skipping transfer tax on direct transfers that skip more than one generation. This has the effect of raising the effective gift and estate tax rates on direct transfers to grandchildren to:

$$(9) \quad \frac{\tau_g}{1+\tau_g} + \frac{\tau_g}{(1+\tau_g)^2}$$

and

(10) $\tau_e + \tau_e(1 - \tau_e)$

respectively. The second term reflects the additional gift and estate taxes levied on generation skipping transfers.

IV.   FISCAL CONTRIBUTION

1.   Revenue yield

In fiscal year 1934, its first full year in effect, gift tax receipts were $9 million. In fiscal year 2006, the most recent year, gift tax receipts were $1.9 billion. Gift tax revenues grew rapidly in the late 1980s and the 1990s, before the slow down experienced in recent years. Trends in receipts since the inception of the tax are summarized in Table 6 and Figure 1.

In fiscal year 1977, which reflects calendar year 1976 transfers, gift tax receipts soared to $2 billion, about five times the receipts in the previous year, an all time high in real terms. At the time, gift taxes accounted for 24 percent of the combined yield of estate and gift tax revenues, well above its historic trend.[24] This surge in receipts reflects the acceleration in gifts made in anticipation of the higher gift tax rates in 1977 brought about by TRA76. This surge may have resulted in lower gift tax receipts in the late 1970s when perhaps these transfers would have taken place absent the changes made by TRA76.

---

[23] Note that this equality will not hold for those with wealth in the graduated tax rate schedule range, as the tax rate increases with (nominal) wealth appreciation.

[24] Note that, prior to 1977, gift tax rates were set at 75 percent of the prevailing estate tax rates. Adjusted for the tax rate differential, the gift tax share stood at 30 percent.

This is not the first time that top wealth holders accelerated inter-vivos transfers. In 1935, estate tax rates were increased mid-year, while corresponding gift tax increases were delayed to the end of the calendar year. The maximum estate tax rate, for instance, was increased from 60 to 70 percent on August 31, 1935. The same legislation, however, increased the maximum gift tax rate from 45 to 52.5 percent (75 percent of the applicable estate tax rate), effective January 1, 1936, four months later. In both fiscal years 1935 and 1936, gift tax receipts stood well above the trend. A similar pattern is also observed in fiscal year 1942, as gift tax rate increases lagged behind estate tax rate increases.[25]

The strong growth in gift tax receipts in the late 1980s may reflect the deferral of gifts in the early 1980s as tax rates were scheduled to decline gradually from 70 percent down to 50 percent in 1985. The surge in revenues in fiscal year 1990 (calendar year 1989 gifts) may also reflect the expiration of the $2 million GSTT exemption per donee at the end of calendar year 1989; transfers accelerated to take advantage of the exemption are fully taxable under the gift tax but avoid the additional GSTT tax. The overall increase in gift taxes may also be explained by the acceleration of spousal bequests in the early 1980s brought about by the introduction of the unlimited marital deduction.[26] The reduction in gifts in recent years may reflect deferrals of transfers induced by the phased-in reduction

[25] The surge in revenues in fiscal year 1973 (calendar year 1972) maybe explained by the acceleration in gifts attributed to the changes in filing requirements introduced by the Excise, Estate, and Gift Adjustment Act of 1970.

[26] A tax minimizing strategy may require a parent to bequeath his non-cash wealth to his surviving spouse, who in turn gifts the stepped up assets to her children, rather then gift them directly. See Joulfaian (2000, 2005). In addition, by increasing spousal bequests in the 1early 1980s, donors may have arranged for future gifts by the surviving spouse when tax rates were lower.

in estate and gift tax rates under EGTRRA, reminiscent of the experience of the early 1980's.

2.   Administration Cost

Little is known about the direct cost of administering the gift tax. Obviously the government incurs some costs in administering the gift tax, including processing of tax returns and enforcement, which reduces the net intake from the tax. In fiscal year 2005, the entire budget of the Internal Revenue Service (IRS) was about $10 billion. The IRS processed about 175 million tax returns, of which only 263,000 were gift tax returns (Table 7).

The gift tax also accounts for a tiny fraction of audited tax returns. In fiscal 2005, the IRS examined 1.3 million tax returns, of which only 2,125 were gift tax returns. The latter resulted in assessments of $671 million in additional taxes, or $315,700 per examined return. Of course the cost of these audits is at least in part offset by their yield and overall contribution to collected revenues. The number of gift tax returns examined has remained steady over the past decade as gleaned from Table 7.

Whether measured as a fraction of all returns filed, or as a fraction of the returns examined, the gift tax seems to account for a fraction well under one percent of the overall number of processed returns. Consequently, it may also account for less than one percent of the IRS budget. Given the interaction with the estate tax, the cost of administering the estate tax may also need to be considered. However, only 74,172 estate tax returns were filed in FY 2005, of which only 6,081 were examined. Again, the combined cost is likely to be a small fraction of the $10 billion budget, and the $28.5 billion in estate and gift tax revenues collected in fiscal year 2006 ($24.5 in FY 2005).[27]

V.   THE TAXPAYERS

1.   Number of Taxpayers

Gift tax returns are required to be filed when the amount transferred, other than that for tuition and medical expenses, exceeds the annual exclusion. Thus, an individual making a gift of $10,000 (indexed) to his son, or a couple making $20,000 (indexed) in split gifts to each of their three children, may not file tax returns. Consequently, the majority of Americans are not subjected to the gift tax or its filing requirements.

In fiscal year 2005, the latest year for which data is available, some 277,000 gift tax returns were filed.[28] The number of tax returns filed grew steadily from fiscal year 1933 through 2005, as shown in Table 8. The number of returns filed peaked at 386,802 in fiscal year 1977, in anticipation of the legislated tax increases to take effect on January 1, 1977. With the anticipated tax rate reductions along with the expansion of the annual exclusion from $3,000 to $10,000 by ERTA81, the number of returns declined significantly in the early 1980's. With economic and population growth, the number

---

[27] In fiscal year 2005, 94,269 FTE's were employed by the IRS (2005 Data book), of which 20211 were engaged in enforcement (http://www.irs.gov/pub/newsroom/11-06_enforcement_stats.pdf).

[28] These include amended returns.

increased over time. The indexing provision of TRA97 and the temporary features of

EGTRRA have kept this growth in check in recent years.[29]

The national trend in filing of federal gift tax returns is mirrored at the state level, most

likely reflecting each jurisdiction's particular tax treatment of gifts and demographics.

Table 9 provides a geographical breakdown of the federal gift tax returns filed over four

decades. The residents of the states of California, Florida, New York, and Texas filed the

greatest number of returns and accounted for 40 percent of the taxpayers. The fastest

growth in the 1990s took place in California, Washington, Texas, Alaska, and New

Jersey.

2.   Frequency of Making Gifts

While Table 8 reports the number of donors over time, an interesting question is whether

these are the same donors making repeated gifts. To address this question one needs

information on all the lifetime gifts made by the wealth holders. Fortunately, such

information is typically reported on estate tax returns, which require the reporting of all

taxable gifts made during life. Joulfaian and McGarry (2004) employ a sample of such

returns for decedents in 1992 together with information on gifts made over several

decades.

In 1992, the applicable estate tax filing threshold was $600,000 in gross assets. The tax

filing requirement for inter-vivos gifts varied over time. In the early years, the threshold

---

[29] The surge, or acceleration, in returns filed in fiscal year 1973 may have been brought about by the

was $4000-$5000. For the years 1943-1981 the threshold was just $3000, and in 1982 it increased to $10,000 as was reported in Section II. Of the sample of 2830 observations studied by Joulfaian and McGarry in which the wealthy are over represented, only 866 estates reported making gifts in excess of the annual exclusion.

Figure 2 reports the relative frequency of giving by donors in the sample in each year from 1936 through 1992. Among those who did, i.e. the 866 estates, the vast majority made gifts towards the very end of life. The fraction of the sample giving rises steadily and peaks at around 35 percent in 1990-1991 when the average age would have been approximately 77. In other words, the probability of making gifts rises with age; the old are more likely to make gifts than the young.

Turning to the question of how many times or how often the wealthy make gifts during their lifetime, Figure 3 reports the distribution of the frequency with which taxable gifts (in excess of $3,000/$10,000) are made. The vast majority of the sample of those who made a taxable inter-vivos gifts, did so in only one year: 28 percent made gifts only once, 15 percent twice (two years), and just 13 percent three times during life.

3.   Gifts Reported on Gift Tax Returns

In fiscal year 2005, and as reported in Table 10, some 261,000 gift tax returns were filed.[30] A total of $23 billion in "taxable" gifts were reported to have been made, i.e. gifts

---

change in filing requirements introduced by Excise, Estate, and Gift Adjustment Act of 1970.

[30] This is smaller than the figure of 276,570 returns reported in Table 8 because it excludes amended and duplicate returns.

in excess of deductions and exemptions. Most of these transfers took place in calendar year 2004. About 94,000 reported zero taxable gifts, while only 7,000 filers reported a positive gift tax liability. A total of $1.6 billion in gift taxes were paid by the latter, for an average of $550,000. About 121,000 taxpayers reported making gifts in prior years totaling $66.6 billion. Of the 16 donors reporting gifts in excess of $20 million in 2005, for instance, 15 also reported making gifts in prior years.

Some 35,000 returns reported valuation discounts, and accounted for about a quarter of the gifts. These discounts were claimed by donors of all sizes, including 14,373 who reported zero taxable gifts. However, large donors seem more likely to claim such discounts.[31]

One remarkable aspect of the figures reported in Table 10 is the sheer number of returns filed with gifts below the annual exclusion. About 37,000 returns with split gifts reported gross transfers below $22,000. Of these 7,341 returns reported positive taxable gifts. Other donors, 10297 exactly, reported gifts below $11,000. About 10 percent of these, or 1402 returns, reported positive taxable gifts.[32] Little of the filing of these returns may be attributable to taxpayer errors given that many had previously filed such returns. This may also potentially be the byproduct of the interplay between aggressive estate planning and the three year gift tax statute of limitations. It may also be explained by gifts of future

---

[31] Recall that TRA97 introduced the three year statute of limitations which runs if a gift was adequately disclosed on a gift tax return.

[32] For the few returns reporting gifts made prior to 2002, an exclusion of $10,000/$20,000 is employed in these calculations. Note that gifts of future interests in property may not benefit from the annual exclusion.

interest which do not benefit from the annual exclusion. Clearly, and given the sheer number of returns filed, this is an area that warrants further study.

4.   Gifts Reported on Estate Tax Returns

Another question of interest is how wealthy are the donors. Table 11 provides summary statistics on the pattern of inter vivos gifts as gleaned from estate tax returns. These returns are for decedents in 1998 with tax returns filed over the years 1998 through 2000. Because the unified nature of estate and gift taxes, and as eluded to earlier, gifts made during life (adjusted taxable gifts) are reported on the estate tax return and added to the taxable estate in determining the estate tax liability.[33]

From a universe of 105,218 estates, only 12,242 or 11.6 percent reported making lifetime taxable gifts. Of the smallest estates, those with estates under $1 million, only 6 percent reported making gifts at any point during life. In contrast, 76 percent for those with estates in excess of $20 million reported making such transfers.

Overall, lifetime gifts represent a small fraction of the gross estate. The average fraction transferred is 2.8 percent for all estates. This ranges from a low of 1.3 percent for estates under $1 million to a high of 3.4 percent for estates in excess of $20 million. Very little is transferred during life.[34]

---

[33] Only the gift tax and value of life insurance for transfers made within three years of the date of death are reported on schedule G, and form part of the gross estate. On these returns, about $53.5 billion was reported on Schedule G by 36,576 estates. Only $386 million was reported as gift tax on 1,011 estates.

[34] It is very likely that lifetime gifts of a particular class of assets are heavily discounted giving rise to the illusion of less generosity.

VI.   BEHAVIORAL EFFECTS

The gift tax, like other taxes, may influence behavior. It may influence the choice

between gifts and bequests, as well as affect the timing of gifts, as gift tax rates change

over time. Gift taxes may also have compliance implications, interstate mobility, among

others.[35]

1.   The Choice between Gifts and Bequests

As we have seen in Section III, there is considerable divergence in the tax treatment of

gifts and bequests. This differential treatment may distort the allocation between the two

modes of transfers. Depending on the wealth holders' circumstances, and the tax regime

in place, lifetime gifts might be the tax preferred mode of transfer. Of course in the

absence of the gift tax, and in the presence of the estate tax and depending on the income

tax regime in place, there will be a greater preference for gifts.

Joulfaian (2000 and 2005) provides evidence on the effects of taxes on the timing of

transfers. In these studies I explore how variations in gift tax rates, along with estate and

capital gains tax rates, influence the choice of transfers. Using a sample of 2355 estate tax

returns of parents who died in 1989, the lifetime share of gifts in total transfers, i.e. gifts

plus bequests, is first computed. Next, a measure of the relative price of gifts is derived

using equations (5) and (7) in Section III. Gift, estate, and capital gains tax rates are

calculated for each individual depending on the size of wealth and state of residency.

The findings show the relative frequency of gifts declines with the tax price of gifts (relative to the price of bequests). The importance of taxes is further explored using multivariate analysis. Results from such analyses are summarized in Table 12 which reports generalized (Heckman) and FIML (standard) Tobit estimates. These show that the share of transfers made during life declines with the gift price. The higher the tax on gifts, the greater is the share of bequests in transfers. The findings suggest that much of the gifts will no longer take place in the absence of the estate and gift taxes.

2.   Timing of Gifts

A. Time series evidence

In addition to the choice between gifts and bequests, the gift tax may also influence the timing of gifts. Donors, for instance, may time their gifts so as to maximize after tax transfers. Taking a casual look at Figure 1, one cannot help but notice the dramatic upsurge in gifts prior to tax increases taking effect. This pattern is repeated prior to virtually every announced increase in gift tax rates in the early 1930s and 1940s, and in 1976. In 1976, for instance, the maximum gift tax rate was expected to increase from 57.75 percent to 70 percent on January 1, 1977. Prior to the effective date, gifts surged and quadrupled. When compared to prior years, however, the pattern following rate reductions, such as those announced in 1981, is flat. But a clearer pattern emerges when gift tax receipts are compared to estate tax receipts. The share of the gift tax in the combined estate and gift tax receipts was one percent in 1981, the year prior to the tax

---

[35] A number of studies address the effect of estate taxation on gifts. See Bernheim et al. (2004), McGarry

cuts taking effect. This compares to 30 percent in calendar 1976, 27 percent in 1941, 51 percent in 1935, and 41 percent in 1934 (Table 6).[36]

While Figure 1 and Table 6 are quite revealing, they tells us little about the strength of the relationship between gifts and taxes. In other words, they don't tell us by how much gifts would change for a given change in the tax treatment of gifts. Joulfaian (2004) employs multivariate analysis to further shed light on the magnitude and timing of the effects of gift taxation. Gift tax receipts (normalized) over the years 1933-1998 are regressed on current, lagged, and expected gift tax prices measured using a predicted gift tax rates. These tax prices are derived using equation (5) from Section III, but without the estate tax recapture. Control variables include (1) the Standard and Poor index, adjusted for inflation, and Real GDP to control for wealth growth and the underlying business cycle, (2) the real amount of the lifetime gift tax exemption to control for the segment of the population potentially subject to the gift tax as well as bracket creep resulting from the lack of indexing the exemption, and (3) and a dummy for 1989 when the GSTT temporary exemption was set to expire, after which generation skipping transfers became subject to an additional tax.

Results from this multivariate analysis are reported in Table 13. Column (1) of Table 13 provides estimates of the determinants of gift tax revenues for the years 1933 through 1998. The estimated coefficient on the current gift tax price is –14.4, with standard error

---

(2000), Page (2003), and Poterba (2001).

[36] Calendar or liability year data roughly translate into fiscal year data lagged by one year. Fiscal year 1977, for instance, becomes 1976 calendar year.

of 2.9. The estimated coefficient on the lagged tax price is also negative, but not precisely measured. On the other hand, the estimated coefficient on the expected tax price is positive with a value of 13.2 (s.e. of 2.6). These estimates suggest that the gift tax price has a depressing effect on gift tax revenues, but that expected increases may boost gift tax revenues in the short run. The transitory elasticity with respect to the gift tax price is about -14.4 (s.e.=2.90), with a permanent elasticity, defined as the sum of the coefficients on the gift price, that is not precisely measured (-3.47 with s.e.=2.34). The estimated transitory elasticity, while large in absolute value, is in harmony with the pattern observed in Figure 1. The results also show that the expiration of the GSTT exemption may have accelerated transfers into 1989. These findings are robust to a number of specifications that consider the effects of the estate tax, or that employ alternative measures of the gift tax rates.[37]

B. Evidence from a sample of estate tax returns

Instead of focusing on aggregate time series data to explore the effects of the gift tax on the timing of gifts, Joulfaian and McGarry (2004) examine the life time gifts of a group of wealthy decedents. More specifically, they employ a sample of estate tax returns of decedents in 1992, and trace the gifts made during 56 years prior to the date of death. This is the very same data employed in generating Figures 2 and 3.

---

[37] The coefficient on the price of bequests is negatively and imprecisely measured in column (2). This becomes positive and significant in the absence of the expected gift tax price. However, the R is reduced from 0.47 to 0.3 in this specification.

In this paper the authors examine how the gift tax influences the probability of making gifts, the amount of gifts made in every year of the sample, as well as how lifetime gifts are allocated over time. A summary of the findings is provided in Table 14, which control for the S&P index, and time/age. Column (1) explores the determinants of the probability of giving during life. The coefficient of the current tax price is -23.3 (se=3.6), suggesting fewer individuals would make gifts when tax rates are high. The coefficient on the expected future tax price is 17.8 (se=3.3), suggesting that more individuals would make gifts if they expected tax rates to rise. This finding points to a very strong transitory effect on making gifts, with a smaller albeit still strong permanent effect.

Column (2) of Table 13 focuses on the amount of gifts reported annually, stated in natural logarithm. The estimated coefficient on the log of the current tax price is -8.4 (se=4.3), while that on the expected price is 8.5 (se=3.9). The gift tax has a large effect on giving in the short run, with an estimated elasticity of -8.4, but the permanent effect is close to zero. A similar conclusion is arrived at when the dependent variable is stated as the share of lifetime gifts made in a given year. The estimated coefficient on the current tax price is -27.7 (se=6.2), while that on the expected price is 30.2 (se=6.47). Gifts also are shown to surge in 1989, as also reported in Table 13, when the temporary GSTT exemption when set to expire. In addition to the tax effects, gifts are also shown to rise over time as donors get older.

Overall, the findings in Joulfaian (2004) and Joulfaian and McGarry (2004) point to a very high transitory response to gift taxation, but with much weaker permanent response.

3. Compliance

The gift tax, like all taxes, is susceptible to leakages due to tax evasion and noncompliance. High gift tax rates may induce donors to understate the amount of gifts made. However, there is little direct evidence on the annual size of noncompliance with the gift tax. The most direct evidence on the magnitude of gift tax evasion can be gleaned from audited estate tax returns. Eller (2001, p. 123), for instance, examines cumulative lifetime gifts reported on audited estate tax returns filed in 1992. She reports that about $200 million, or roughly 20 percent, of gifts are underreported.[38]

An alternative strategy is to employ survey data to gauge the size of gifts escaping gift taxation. Using such survey data, Feinstein (1999) concludes that "the IRS collected approximately one billion in gift taxes in 1992, but extrapolations from HRS and AHEAD data indicate that households most likely owed more than three billion in taxes." Later, Feinstein and Ho (1999) revise these estimates by discounting transfers for tuition and medical expenses, and conclude that about one half, instead of two-thirds, is evaded.

Table 15 replicates the distribution of total gifts reported in the HRS/AHEAD survey data employed by Feinstein and Ho. Using the HRS data for 1992/1993 yields a population estimate of 15 million individuals making total gifts of $45.8 billion. Of these, however, only 375,000 individuals made gifts in excess of $10,000 per recipient, for a total value of $6.5 billion. It is noteworthy that taxable gifts, i.e. those in excess of the annual

$10,000 exclusion, are well below the $600,000 exempted by virtue of the unified credit. In other words, it is most likely that the entire population in the HRS/AHEAD data paid zero gift taxes and not the $2-3 billion reported earlier in Feinstein and Ho.

In contrast to survey data, tax return data contain limited information on transfers as only those with transfers in excess of the annual exclusion are required to file. The data on gift tax returns filed for transfers made in 1993, reported in the right panel of Table 15, show a total of 208,307 tax returns with total gifts of $23.9 billion, or taxable gifts of $17 billion made by just 138,000 individuals. Of the latter, about 5,800 reported gross gifts in excess of $600,000 each, for a total of roughly $4.5 billion in gifts subject to tax well above the zero amounts observed in the survey data.

Table 15 makes it clear that survey data, and in particular the HRS/AHEAD data, fail to point to a significant noncompliance with the gift tax. Indeed, the findings in Feinstein and Ho may have resulted from overlooking the unified credit which exempted $600,000 of lifetime gifts in 1992.[39]

While there is limited evidence on the size of noncompliance with the gift tax, anecdotal evidence points to a serious tax avoidance problem particularly in the area of valuation discounts. Indeed, at times the line between noncompliance and tax avoidance is blurred. Assets transferred are supposed to reflect the market or the appraised value. Often,

---

[38] Using the same data, Eller et al (2001) explored how the marginal estate tax rate affects the reporting of the estate tax liability.

transfers of fractional interest in a property are valued at a discount. For instance, it is not uncommon to claim a minority discount in valuing gifts of closely held businesses among other assets.[40] Amazing as it may sound, some claim a discount on cash transfers if these are rolled into a family limited partnership, and a minority interest is transferred. While little research is undertaken to explore the size and scope of such valuation practices, these undermine the gift as well as estate tax bases.

In fiscal year 2005, and as noted earlier, an assessment of addition taxes of $671 million was levied on gift tax returns examined (see Table 7), for an average assessment of $316,000. The potential additional tax may very well be much larger as less than one percent of tax returns are audited. However, little can be said about how under reporting of gifts responds to changes in tax regimes. Undoubtedly, the interplay between the statute of limitations introduced in TRA97 and the low audit coverage of "exempt" gifts creates ample opportunities for noncompliance.

4.   Other

In addition to the effects of the gift tax on the optimal mode and timing of transfers, the tax is also likely to have other economic consequences that are yet to be explored. It may, for instance, counteract the incentives for transfers created by the income tax, induce charitable contributions during life, and exacerbate interstate competition for the wealthy, among other effects.

---

[39] These survey data do not contain households with sufficient wealth to adequately address compliance patterns of the super rich.

[40] The average discount is about 30 percent of the "value" of the gift. See Eller (2004, pp. 59-60).

a.   Transfers to Recipients Facing Lower Tax Rates

Graduated income tax rates have long been thought to create incentives for the transfer of wealth from the well off to the less well off children or to multiple trusts created on their behalf.[41] The return on the underlying assets would be taxed at a tax rate lower than that of the donor, for a significant saving in taxes. The gift tax, by offsetting the tax savings from income shifting, reduces income tax motivated transfers and "estate splitting" as the proponents of the introduction of the gift tax in 1932 had argued.

Consider a parent wishing to transfer wealth W with return r, in the presence of income tax rate of τ_p and τ_c for wealthy parent and low income child (or trust on her behalf), respectively. Assuming away transfer taxes for now, if wealth is held and transferred at death, in period n, than the child receives $W[1+r(1-\tau_p)]^n$. If the parent instead gifts W, than the child will have wealth of $W[1+r(1-\tau_c)]^n$ in period n. As long as the child or trust income tax rate is lower than that of the parent, i.e., $\tau_c < \tau_p$, gifts will be preferred as $W[1+r(1-\tau_p)]^n < W[1+r(1-\tau_c)]^n$. In the presence of the gift tax, with a tax rate of τ_g, a lifetime transfer of W yields the child a much smaller wealth of $1/(1+\tau_g)W[1+r(1-\tau_c)]^n$.[42]

While the introduction of the gift tax may offset the incentives created by progressive income taxation, or capital income taxation in general, there is no empirical evidence to

---

[41] By creating multiple trusts, a transfer is split into smaller amounts yielding streams of little income to each trust so that each is taxed at the lower rates of graduated tax rate schedules.

[42] A graduate tax rate schedule complicates the computations, but should yield a similar qualitative outcome. While the gift tax may make income shifting less attractive, the estate tax may tip the balance in favor of gifts.

date on the effects of the gift tax on such transfers. However, the compression of the tax rate schedule that applies to the income of trusts, introduced by TRA86 and modified in subsequent legislations, eliminates the income tax savings from lifetime gifts via trusts. Indeed, while the 35 percent maximum income tax rate applies to individuals with taxable income in excess of $336,550 in 2006 (single or married), it applies to taxable incomes of trusts in excess of only $10,050, thus eliminating much of the income tax incentives for estate splitting by creating a large number of trusts.

b.   Charitable Contributions

The effects of deductibility of charitable contributions under the income tax are well documented and thoroughly analyzed (Randolph, 1995; Auten at al., 2002). The effects of the estate tax on these lifetime contributions have also been explored (Auten and Joulfaian, 1996; Joulfaian, 2001). The latter findings suggest that the estate tax has a positive, albeit small, effect on contributions. There are no studies to date that address the effects of the gift tax itself. One is tempted to borrow from the findings in literature on the estate tax (Joulfaian, 2000b). This might be a reasonable approach if one were to assume that the parent or donor is indifferent between the timing of gifts and bequests.[43]

c.   Interstate Competition for the Wealthy

The federal estate tax structure is designed so as to minimize interstate competition for the wealthy. The federal estate tax credit for state death taxes was introduced in 1925 as a counter measure for the initiative by a number of states to abolish inheritance taxes in an attempt to attract the wealthy away from other states.[44] With a rate schedule of up to 16

percent of the taxable estate, the credit offsets much of the state inheritance tax liabilities

of the very wealthy. In contrast, however, no such provision is available under the gift tax

fully exposing differences is state tax rates.[45]

Because gifts take place during life, there are likely to be greater opportunities to plan

around the gift tax. Certainly the donor has greater control on the timing and disposition

of gifts than bequests. The donor, for instance, may "temporarily" move to another state

with lower or no gift taxes. However, there is no empirical evidence on the effects of the

gift tax on the mobility of the wealthy. One may borrow form the literature on the effects

of the estate tax with its mixed evidence,[46] but then, once again, the overreaching

assumption has to be made that the donor is indifferent between gifts and bequests.

VII. CONCLUSION

The gift tax has evolved since its inception in 1932. The tax base, the rate structure, and

how the gift tax interacts with the income and estate taxes underwent a number of

changes over the past seven decades. Yet its primary role as a measure to protect the

estate and income tax bases from erosion remains its salient feature. The compression of

---

[43] This may not be fully consistent with the fact that the wealthy give so little of their wealth in the form of lifetime gifts (see Table 11).

[44] The tax credit reflected the federal government's intention to have states adopt taxes "... equivalent to 25% of the federal tax" (Treasury Report for 1924, p. 11). The intent here was to impose uniform state inheritance taxes and minimize interstate competition for the wealthy (Schultz, 1926, p. 161-2).

[45] Actually, only (1-e), the net federal estate tax rate, is paid to the extent that lifetime state gift taxes reduce the size of the taxable estate.

[46] See Conway and Rork (2006) and Bakija and Slemrod (2004), for example.

the tax rate schedule of estates and trusts, and the gradual reduction in income tax rates brought about by repeated tax reforms over the years has reduced the efficacy of gift tax as a protective measure. However, the gift tax will continue to play that role in the presence of progressive income taxation and as long as capital income is taxed. Equally important, is that the viability of the estate tax cannot be assured in the absence of the gift tax.

While the gift tax is critical in preempting the erosion of the income and estate taxes, a number of its features need to be re-examined. There seems to be a lack of coordination between the income tax and the gift tax, or the estate tax for that matter. In particular, the rate structures share little in common. The maximum ordinary income tax rate is 35 percent (15 percent for capital gains), for instance, compared to 55 percent for each of the gift and estate taxes. Also the tax exclusive nature of the gift tax sets it apart from the estate tax.

Notwithstanding its protective nature, the gift tax itself is undermined by a number of valuation practices that weaken much of its efficacy. These practices drastically narrow the base of a tax that is saddled with high marginal tax rates. This combination has the potential of biasing choices and distorting donor behavior.

References

Auten, Gerald, Holger Sieg, and Charles T. Clotfelter, "Charitable Giving, Income and Taxes: An Analysis of Panel Data," American Economic Review 92, March 2002, 371-382.

Auten, Gerald, and David Joulfaian. "Charitable Contributions and Intergenerational Transfers," Journal of Public Economics 59:1, January 1996, 55-68.

Bakija, Jon and Joel Slemrod. "Do the Rich Flee from High State Taxes? Evidence from Federal Estate Tax Returns," National Bureau of Economic Research Working Paper 10645, 2004.

Bernheim, Douglas B., Robert J. Lemke, and John Karl Scholz. "Do Estate and Gift Taxes Affect the Timing of Private Transfers?" Journal of Public Economics 88:12, December 2004, 2617-34.

Conway, Karen Smith, and Jonathan C. Rork, State "Death Taxes and Elderly Migration – The Chicken or the Egg?" National Tax Journal 59: 1, March 2006, 97-128.

Eller, Martha Britton. "Inter Vivos Wealth Transfers, 1997 Gifts," Statistics of Income Bulletin, Winter 2003 – 2004, Publication 1136, 2004.

Eller, Martha Britton. "Audit Revaluation of Federal Estate Tax Returns, 1992," Statistics of Income Bulletin, Winter 2000-2001, Publication 1136, 2001.

Eller, Martha Britton, Brian Erard, and Chih-Chin Ho. "Noncompliance with the Federal Estate Tax," in Rethinking Estate and Gift Taxation, William G. Gale, James R. Hines Jr., and Joel Slemrod, editors, the Brookings Institution, Washington, DC, 2001, 375-410.

Feinstein, Jonathan. "Approaches for Estimating Noncompliance: Examples from Federal Taxation in the United States," The Economic Journal, Vol. 109, No. 456, June, 1999, 360-369.

Feinstein, Jonathan, and Chih-Chin Ho, "Predicting Estate Tax Filings and Taxable Gifts," United States Department of the Treasury, Internal Revenue Service, The IRS Research Bulletin, Publication 1500 (Rev. 11-99), 1999, 39-45.

Harriss, C. Lowell, Gift Taxation in the United States," American Council on Public Affairs, Washington, DC, 1940.

House of Representatives, The Revenue Bill of 1932, 7th Congress, 1st Session, Report No. 708, 1932.

Joulfaian, David. "Charitable Giving in Life and at Death," in William G. Gale, James R. Hines, Jr., and Joel Slemrod (eds.), Rethinking Estate and Gift Taxation, Brookings Institutions, 2001, 350-374.

Joulfaian, David. "Choosing Between Gifts and Bequests: How Taxes Affect the Timing of Wealth Transfers," Journal of Public Economics 89:11-12, December, 2005, 2069-2091.

Joulfaian, David. "Choosing Between Gifts and Bequests: How Taxes Affect the Timing of Wealth Transfers," OTA Paper 86, May 2000a.

Joulfaian, David. "Gift Taxes and Lifetime Transfers: Time Series Evidence," Journal of Public Economics, 88:9-10, August, 2004, 1917-1929.

Joulfaian, David. "Estates Taxes and Charitable Bequests by the Wealthy," National Bureau of Economic Research Working Paper no. 7663, April 2000b.

Joulfaian, David. "The Federal Estate and Gift tax: Description, Profile of Taxpayers, and Economic Consequences," OTA Paper 80, U.S. Department of the Treasury, December 1998, www.treas.gov/ota/ota80.pdf.

Joulfaian, David. "Charitable Bequests and Estate Taxes," National Tax Journal 44:2, June 1991, 169-180.

Joulfaian, David and Kathleen McGarry. "Estate and Gift Tax Incentives and Inter Vivos Giving," National Tax Journal, 57:2, Part 2, June 2004, 429-444

McGarry, Kathleen. "Inter Vivos Transfers or Bequests? Estate Taxes and the Timing of Parental Giving," Tax Policy and the Economy 14, 2000, 93-121.

Page, Benjamin R. "Bequest Taxes, Inter Vivos Gifts, and the Bequest Motive," Journal of Public Economics 87:5-6, May 2003, 1219-29.

Poterba, James. "Estate and Gift Taxes and Incentives for Inter Vivos Giving in the United States," Journal of Public Economics 79:1, January 2001, 237-264.

Randolph, William C. "Dynamic Income, Progressive Taxes, and the Timing of Charitable Contributions," Journal of Political Economy 103 No. 4, August, 1995, 709-738.

Roosevelt, Franklin D. The Public Papers and Addresses, v.4, Random House, New York, 1938: 313-14.

Shultz, William J. The Taxation of Inheritance, Houghton Mifflin, The Riverside Press, New York City, 1926.

United States Department of the Treasury, Treasury Report for 1924, Washington, DC.

Table 1

Changes in Estate and Gift Tax Rates

Estate Tax Changes		Gift Tax Changes	
Dates in Effect	Description	Dates in Effect	Description
June 6, 1932	Maximum estate tax rate raised from 20 to 45 percent, effective after 5pm.	June 6, 1932	Gift tax enacted with a maximum rate of 33.75 percent.
May 11, 1934	Rate increased to 60 percent. Act of May 10, 1934.	Jan.1, 1935	Rate increased to 45 percent.
Aug. 31, 1935	Rates increased to 70 percent. Act of August 30, 1935.	Jan.1, 1936	Rate increased to 52.50 percent.
June 26, 1940	Temporary10 percent surtax. Enacted June 25, 1940; and effective through 1945.	June 26, 1940	Same as estate tax.
Sep. 21, 1941	Maximum rate set to 77 percent. Act of September 20, 1941.	Jan. 1, 1942	Rate increased to 57.75 percent.
Oct. 22, 1942	Estate tax exemption increased. Enacted October 21, 1942.	Jan. 1, 1943	Gift tax exemption reduced.
Jan. 1, 1977	Rate reduced to 70 percent. Enacted on October 4, 1976.	Jan. 1, 1977	Estate and gift tax unified, and maximum gift tax rate increased to 70 percent.
Jan. 1, 1982	Maximum rate reduced from 70 percent to 50 percent over 4 years (1982-1985). Unlimited deduction for spousal transfers. Enacted on August 31, 1981.	Jan. 1, 1982	Same as estate tax.
Jan.1, 1985	Maximum rate frozen at 55 percent by legislation enacted on July 18, 1984.	Jan.1, 1985	Same as estate tax.
Oct. 23, 1986	Generation skipping tax introduced, with a temporary $2 million exemption per donee through 1989. Enacted on October 22, 1986.	Sep. 26, 1985	Same as estate tax, but retroactive to 1985.
Jan. 1, 1988	Maximum rate again frozen at 55 percent. Enacted on December 22, 1987.	Jan. 1, 1988	Same as estate tax.
Jan. 1, 1993	Maximum rate set at 55 percent permanently. Enacted on August 10, 1993.	Jan. 1, 1993	Same as estate tax.
Jan 1, 2002	Maximum rate reduced in steps to 45 percent, and tax repealed in 2010, to be reintroduced in 2011.* Enacted June 7, 2001.	Jan. 1, 2002	Maximum rate reduced in steps to 35 percent, and reset to 55 percent in 2011.*

* See Table 5 for temporary rates in effect in 2002 through 2010.

Table 2

Evolution of the Gift Tax Rate Schedule (%)

Wealth ($1,000s)		1932-1934	1935	1936	1940	1942	1977	1982	1983	1984-2011*
From	To									
0	5	0.75	0.75	1.50	1.65	2.25	18.00	18.00	18.00	18.00
5	10	0.75	0.75	1.50	1.65	5.25	18.00	18.00	18.00	18.00
10	20	1.50	1.50	3.00	3.30	8.25	20.00	20.00	20.00	20.00
20	30	2.25	2.25	4.50	4.95	10.50	22.00	22.00	22.00	22.00
30	40	3.00	3.00	6.00	6.60	13.50	22.00	22.00	22.00	22.00
40	50	3.75	3.75	7.50	8.25	16.50	24.00	24.00	24.00	24.00
50	60	5.00	5.25	9.00	9.90	18.75	24.00	24.00	24.00	24.00
60	70	5.00	5.25	9.00	9.90	21.00	26.00	26.00	26.00	26.00
70	80	5.00	6.75	10.50	11.55	21.00	26.00	26.00	26.00	26.00
80	100	5.00	6.75	10.50	11.55	21.00	28.00	28.00	28.00	28.00
100	150	6.50	9.00	12.75	14.03	22.50	30.00	30.00	30.00	30.00
150	200	6.50	9.00	12.75	14.03	22.50	32.00	32.00	32.00	32.00
200	250	8.00	12.00	15.00	16.50	22.50	32.00	32.00	32.00	32.00
250	400	8.00	12.00	15.00	16.50	24.00	34.00	34.00	34.00	34.00
400	500	9.50	14.25	17.25	18.98	24.00	34.00	34.00	34.00	34.00
500	600	9.50	14.25	17.25	18.98	26.25	37.00	37.00	37.00	37.00
600	750	11.00	16.50	19.50	21.45	26.25	37.00	37.00	37.00	37.00
750	800	11.00	16.50	19.50	21.45	27.75	39.00	39.00	39.00	39.00
800	1,000	12.50	18.75	21.75	23.93	27.75	39.00	39.00	39.00	39.00
1,000	1,250	14.00	21.00	24.00	26.40	29.25	41.00	41.00	41.00	41.00
1,250	1,500	14.00	21.00	24.00	26.40	31.50	43.00	43.00	43.00	43.00
1,500	2,000	15.50	23.25	26.25	28.88	33.75	45.00	45.00	45.00	45.00
2,000	2,500	17.00	25.50	28.50	31.35	36.75	49.00	49.00	49.00	49.00
2,500	3,000	18.50	27.75	30.75	33.83	39.75	53.00	53.00	53.00	53.00
3,000	3,500	20.00	30.00	33.00	36.30	42.00	57.00	57.00	57.00	55.00
3,500	4,000	21.50	32.25	35.25	38.78	44.25	61.00	61.00	60.00	55.00
4,000	4,500	23.00	34.50	37.50	41.25	47.25	65.00	65.00	60.00	55.00
4,500	5,000	24.50	36.00	39.75	43.73	47.25	69.00	65.00	60.00	55.00
5,000	6,000	26.00	37.50	42.00	46.20	50.25	70.00	65.00	60.00	55.00
6,000	7,000	27.50	39.00	44.25	48.68	52.50	70.00	65.00	60.00	55.00
7,000	8,000	29.00	40.50	45.75	50.33	54.75	70.00	65.00	60.00	55.00
8,000	9,000	30.50	42.00	47.25	51.98	57.00	70.00	65.00	60.00	55.00
9,000	10,000	32.00	43.50	48.75	53.63	57.00	70.00	65.00	60.00	55.00
10,000	20,000	33.50	45.00	50.50	55.55	57.75	70.00	65.00	60.00	55.00
20,000	50,000	33.50	45.00	51.75	56.93	57.75	70.00	65.00	60.00	55.00
50,000	Over	33.50	45.00	52.50	57.75	57.75	70.00	65.00	60.00	55.00

* See Table 5 for temporary rates in effect in 2002 through 2010.

Table 3

Historical Features of The Gift Tax

Year	Tax Rate Range	Annual Exclusion per donee	Exemption or Equivalent Amount	Unified Credit	Maximum Marital Deduction
1924	1 - 25%	$500	$40,000	N.A.	N.A.
1926	N.A.	N.A.	N.A.	N.A.	N.A.
1932	0.75 - 33.5	5,000	50,000	N.A.	N.A.
1934	0.75 - 45	5,000	50,000	N.A.	N.A.
1936	1.5 - 52.5	5,000	40,000	N.A.	N.A.
1942	2.25 - 57.75	4,000	40,000	N.A.	N.A.
1943	2.25 - 57.75	3,000	30,000	N.A.	N.A.
1949	2.25 - 57.75	3,000	30,000	N.A.	50 % of Gift
1955	2.25 - 57.75	3,000	30,000	N.A.	50 % of Gift
1977	18 - 70	3,000	120,667	$30,000	50 % of Gift
1978	18 - 70	3,000	134,000	34,000	50 % of Gift
1979	18 - 70	3,000	147,333	38,000	50 % of Gift
1980	18 - 70	3,000	161,563	42,000	50 % of Gift
1981	18 - 70	3,000	175,625	47,000	50 % of Gift
1982	18 - 65	10,000	225,000	62,800	100 %
1983	18 - 60	10,000	275,000	79,300	100 %
1984	18 - 55	10,000	325,000	96,300	100 %
1985	18 - 55	10,000	400,000	121,800	100 %
1986	18 - 55	10,000	500,000	155,800	100 %
1987	18 - 55	10,000	600,000	192,800	100 %
1996	18 - 55	10,000	600,000	192,800	100 %
1998	18 - 55	10,000*	625,000	202,050	100 %
1999	18 - 55	10,000*	650,000	211,300	100 %
2000	18 - 55	10,000*	675,000	220,550	100 %
2001	18 - 55	10,000*	675,000	220,550	100 %
2011	18 - 55	Indexed	1,000,000	345,800	100 %

Note: Year reflects period when feature took effect. See Table 5 for temporary provisions in effect for 2002-2010.
* The inflation adjustment is rounded down to the nearest $1,000. In other words, the exemption increases in $1,000 increments. For the years 2002 through 2005, the exemption was set at $11,000. This increased to $12,000 in 2006.

Table 4

Historical Features of the Generation Skipping Transfer Tax

Year	Transfers from Trusts		Direct Transfers		
	Maximum Tax Rate*	Exemption per "donor"	Tax Rate (%)	Exemption per donor	Exemption per donee
1916	N.A.	N.A.	N.A.	N.A.	N.A.
1977	0.70	$250,000	N.A.	N.A.	N.A.
1982	0.65	$250,000	N.A.	N.A.	N.A.
1983	0.60	$250,000	N.A.	N.A.	N.A.
1984	0.55	$250,000	N.A.	N.A.	N.A.
1985	0.55	$250,000	N.A.	N.A.	N.A.
1986	0.55	1,000,000	55	$1,000,000	$2,000,000
1990	0.55	1,000,000	55	1,000,000	N.A.
1999	0.55	1,010,000	55	1,010,000	N.A.
2000	0.55	1,030,000	55	1,030,000	N.A.
2001	0.55	1,060,000	55	1,060,000	N.A.
2011	0.55	Indexed	55	Indexed	N.A.

Note: Year reflects period when feature took effect. 1998 is the base year for indexing. See Table 5 for temporary provisions in effect during 2002-2010.

* Maximum estate tax rate after TRA86.

Table 5

Temporary Provisions of the Estate and Gift Tax: 2002-2010

Year	Estate Tax Rate Range	Exemption or Equivalent Amount	GST Exemption	Gift Tax Rate Range*	Gift Tax Exemption or Equivalent Amount
2002	18 - 50	1,000,000	1,100,000	18 - 50	1,000,000
2003	18 - 49	1,000,000	1,120,000	18 - 49	1,000,000
2004	18 - 48	1,500,000	1,500,000	18 - 48	1,000,000
2005	18 - 47	1,500,000	1,500,000	18 - 47	1,000,000
2006	18 - 46	2,000,000	2,000,000	18 - 46	1,000,000
2007	18 - 45	2,000,000	2,000,000	18 - 45	1,000,000
2008	18 - 45	2,000,000	2,000,000	18 - 45	1,000,000
2009	18 - 45	3,500,000	3,500,000	18 - 45	1,000,000
2010	Repealed	Repealed	Repealed	18 - 35	1,000,000

* Range identical to that of the lower brackets in the last column of Table 2.

Table 6

Gift and Estate Tax Revenues: Fiscal Years 1933-2006
($millions)

Fiscal Year	Gift Tax	Estate Tax	Gift Tax Share	Gift Tax Share*	Fiscal Year	Gift Tax	Estate Tax	Gift Tax Share	Gift Tax Share*
1933	5	30	0.14	0.18	1970	439	3,205	0.12	0.15
1934	9	104	0.08	0.10	1971	432	3,303	0.12	0.15
1935	72	140	0.34	0.41	1972	363	5,073	0.07	0.09
1936	160	219	0.42	0.49	1973	637	4,280	0.13	0.17
1937	24	282	0.08	0.10	1974	441	4,594	0.09	0.11
1938	35	382	0.08	0.11	1975	375	4,236	0.08	0.11
1939	28	332	0.08	0.10	1976	432	4,784	0.08	0.11
1940	29	324	0.08	0.11	1977	1,776	5,551	0.24	0.30
1941	52	351	0.13	0.16	1978	139	5,146	0.03	0.03
1942	92	328	0.22	0.27	1979	175	5,236	0.03	0.03
1943	33	408	0.07	0.10	1980	216	6,173	0.03	0.03
1944	38	469	0.07	0.10	1981	216	6,571	0.03	0.03
1945	47	590	0.07	0.10	1982	108	7,883	0.01	0.01
1946	47	621	0.07	0.09	1983	149	5,904	0.02	0.02
1947	70	701	0.09	0.12	1984	152	5,858	0.03	0.03
1948	77	813	0.09	0.11	1985	276	6,146	0.04	0.04
1949	61	719	0.08	0.10	1986	381	6,577	0.05	0.05
1950	49	649	0.07	0.09	1987	503	6,990	0.07	0.07
1951	91	617	0.13	0.16	1988	426	7,168	0.06	0.06
1952	83	735	0.10	0.13	1989	829	7,916	0.09	0.09
1953	107	774	0.12	0.16	1990	2,128	9,372	0.19	0.19
1954	72	862	0.08	0.10	1991	1,236	9,903	0.11	0.11
1955	88	836	0.10	0.12	1992	1,044	10,099	0.09	0.09
1956	113	1,048	0.10	0.13	1993	1,436	11,141	0.11	0.11
1957	125	1,240	0.09	0.12	1994	2,089	13,136	0.14	0.14
1958	134	1,259	0.10	0.12	1995	1,792	12,971	0.12	0.12
1959	117	1,216	0.09	0.11	1996	2,191	14,998	0.13	0.13
1960	187	1,419	0.12	0.15	1997	2,709	17,136	0.14	0.14
1961	171	1,725	0.09	0.12	1998	3,289	20,787	0.14	0.14
1962	239	1,777	0.12	0.15	1999	4,646	23,136	0.17	0.17
1963	216	1,951	0.10	0.13	2000	4,023	24,926	0.14	0.14
1964	305	2,089	0.13	0.16	2001	3,883	24,441	0.14	0.14
1965	291	2,425	0.11	0.14	2002	1,626	24,813	0.06	0.06
1966	447	2,619	0.15	0.19	2003	1,892	19,990	0.09	0.09
1967	286	2,692	0.10	0.12	2004	1,400	23,397	0.06	0.06
1968	372	2,679	0.12	0.16	2005	1,981	22,813	0.08	0.08
1969	393	3,098	0.11	0.14	2006	1,933	26,755	0.07	0.07

*Adjusts for the gift tax rate that was set at 75 percent of the estate tax rates before calendar year 1977.
Source: Joulfaian (1998), Data Book (various years), and unpublished statistics.

Table 7

Tax Administration Cost
(Amounts in $000s)

	Total	Gift Tax	Estate Tax
IRS Budget (FY 2005)	$10,027,262	n.a.	n.a.
Returns filed (CY 2004)	174,364,531	262,164	74,172
Returns Examined (FY 2005)	1,328,712	2,125	6,081
Percent Examined	0.8	0.8	8.2
Additional Tax Assessed (FY 2005)	$48,622,798	$670,901	$970,091
Per Return Examined	$36.6	$315.7	$159.5

Addendum:

Fiscal Year	Gift Tax Returns Examined	Additional Tax Assessed ($000s)
1988	1,518	240,807
1989	1,277	409,437
1990	1,636	246,775
1991	1,704	140,902
1992	2,071	193,849
1993	2,120	202,009
1994	n.a.	n.a.
1995	1,893	201,603
1996	1,924	350,680
1997	2,085	375,004
1998	2,010	367,035
1999	2,369	346,061
2000	2,097	459,785
2001	2,005	343,279
2002	1,899	405,047
2003	1,855	488,923
2004	1,979	546,442
2005	2,125	670,901
2006	2,051	504,731

Source: IRS Commissioner's Annual Report (various years) and Data Book (various years).

Table 8

Number of Gift Tax Returns Filed: Fiscal Years 1933-2005

Fiscal Year	Number	Fiscal Year	Number
1933	1,710	1970	147,693
1934	3,619	1971	165,481
1935	11,410	1972	190,743
1936	22,590	1973	243,895
1937	17,046	1974	252,653
1938	16,601	1975	260,094
1939	13,614	1976	302,464
1940	14,435	1977	386,802
1941	17,369	1978	195,194
1942	30,048	1979	201,785
1943	23,872	1980	215,993
1944	20,772	1981	198,620
1945	22,939	1982	99,533
1946	23,554	1983	90,098
1947	27,046	1984	87,216
1948	30,603	1985	94,610
1949	27,330	1986	102,965
1950	32,155	1987	104,627
1951	39,585	1988	102,569
1952	45,656	1989	121,294
1953	49,000	1990	146,014
1954	48,000	1991	154,966
1955	58,000	1992	167,680
1956	68,000	1993	211,363
1957	77,000	1994	214,302
1958	79,520	1995	215,010
1959	85,080	1996	226,334
1960	91,132	1997	250,842
1961	93,581	1998	257,722
1962	95,874	1999	285,641
1963	100,020	2000	304,558
1964	107,172	2001	304,079
1965	121,517	2002	278,926
1966	133,646	2003	287,456
1967	136,729	2004	249,019
1968	138,514	2005	276,570
1969	150,785	2006	25,5651

Source: IRS Commissioner's Annual Report (various years) and Data Book (various years).

Table 9

Gift Tax Returns Filed by State in Select Fiscal Years

	1971	1981	1991	2001
Alabama	1,996	2336	1871	3,536
Alaska	72	252	183	422
Arizona	1,446	2009	1673	4,092
Arkansas	1,294	1833	1021	1,730
California	13,647	13,356	13,311	27,373
Colorado	2,368	3414	2191	5,839
Connecticut	3,958	4417	4223	10,219
Delaware	655	667	606	941
Florida	8,272	9703	12,170	23,706
Georgia	3,277	4381	3121	7,761
Hawaii	824	1832	1258	1,654
Idaho	584	816	394	1,010
Illinois	10,377	10,791	7,111	13,149
Indiana	3,436	4760	2736	5,663
Iowa	3,166	5977	1733	2,734
Kansas	3,093	3,962	1,737	3,150
Kentucky	1,806	2259	1622	3,659
Louisiana	1,751	2178	1314	2,598
Maine	632	985	845	1,517
Maryland & DC	3,960	4371	3552	6,904
Massachusetts	5,272	5782	5663	10,676
Michigan	5,495	5562	5377	8,835
Minnesota	2,609	5557	4497	7,141
Mississippi	1,200	1403	869	1,533
Missouri	3,842	4128	2648	5,785
Montana	1,233	2043	767	1,383
Nebraska	2,659	4300	1552	2,170
Nevada	443	608	665	1,720
New Hampshire	606	868	941	2,040
New Jersey	5,859	5342	5198	11,431
New Mexico	721	846	597	1,068
New York	19,265	16,108	14,909	24,476
North Carolina	3,430	4496	3620	7,825
North Dakota	712	2002	723	967
Ohio	7,476	7,973	7,318	12,182
Oklahoma	2,635	3339	1591	2,393
Oregon	1,851	2916	1930	3,830
Pennsylvania	6,691	6,801	6,551	13,850
Rhode Island	590	631	648	1,297
South Carolina	1,334	2117	1642	3,600
South Dakota	825	1844	673	961
Tennessee	2,103	2389	2168	4,370
Texas	9,795	10,882	9,514	20,697
Utah	721	1707	641	1,153
Vermont	396	584	359	714
Virginia	3,219	4649	3649	7,423
Washington	2,021	2,724	2,516	6,827
West Virginia	841	917	604	1,123
Wisconsin	3,979	8509	3622	7,286
Wyoming	529	940	485	893
International	515	354	357	773
Total	165,481	198,620	154,966	304,079

Source: IRS Commissioner's Annual Report (various years) and Data Book (various years).

47

Table 10

Gifts Reported on Gift Tax Returns Filed in Fiscal Year 2005
(Amounts in $1,000s)

Current Gifts* ($1,000s)		Current Gifts*		Gift Tax on Current Gifts		Past Gifts	
		Returns	Amount	Returns	Amount	Returns	Amount
Zero		94,035	0	0	0	39,157	18,844,166
1 -	10	34,599	158,967	734	1,204	21,927	9,100,125
10 -	200	100,196	6,728,129	2,609	79,650	47,271	23,192,790
200 -	1,000	31,467	13,211,855	2,605	362,965	11,881	10,003,351
1,000 -	2,500	811	1,158,540	809	348,020	544	2,475,431
2,500 -	5,000	172	597,176	172	265,789	163	1,536,189
5,000 -	10,000	57	400,482	57	185,587	53	634,895
10,000 -	20,000	17	213,450	17	102,419	15	272,001
20,000 and over		16	547,869	16	268,508	15	549,045
All		261,370	23,016,469	7,018	1,605,276	121,024	66,607,993
Returns with Valuation Discounts Only							
Zero		14,373	0	0	0	5,888	3,761,293
1 -	10	4,124	13,894	151	207	3,080	2,207,461
10 -	200	9,400	778,668	317	9,350	5,566	3,092,551
200 -	1,000	6,603	3,195,076	534	60,816	3,200	1,742,656
1,000 -	2,500	224	312,955	224	85,438	146	283,427
2,500 -	5,000	47	163,985	47	72,329	45	509,326
5,000 -	10,000	12	87,397	12	40,516	11	110,699
10,000 -	20,000	5	76,237	5	36,558	5	30,166
20,000 and over		9	325,515	9	156,031	9	429,678
All		34,797	4,953,727	1,299	461,245	17,950	12,167,257
Returns with Split Gifts Below the Annual Exclusion ($22,000)**							
Zero		29,227	0	0	0	8,895	1,621,789
1 -	20	7,341	41,593	40	25	3,513	606,385
All		36,568	41,593	40	25	12,408	2,228,174
Returns with Gifts (not Split) Below the Annual Exclusion ($11,000)**							
Zero		8,895	0	0	0	1,848	227,629
1 -	10	1,402	5,184	8	0	817	37,202
All		10,297	5,184	8	0	2,665	264,831

* Gifts exclusive of gift tax, less exemptions and deductions, from Form 709, Schedule A, Part 4, Line 11.
** The appropriate amount should reflect the number of recipients.

Source: Author's calculations based on gift tax returns filed in fiscal year 2005, and primarily reflect gifts made in 2004.

Table 11

Gifts Reported on Estate Tax Returns of Decedents in 1998
(Amounts in $millions)

Size of Wealth [a] ($000s)		All Estates		Taxable Gifts Reported on Estate Tax Returns [b]			
From	To	Number	Wealth Amount	Number	Percent of Returns	Gift Amount	Percent of Wealth
Under	1,000	55,478	41,769	3,433	6.19	559	1.34
1,000	1,500	22,656	27,601	2,070	9.14	559	2.02
1,500	2,000	9,806	16,824	1,444	14.73	362	2.15
2,000	2,500	4,986	11,091	1,004	20.14	338	3.05
2,500	5,000	7,909	26,826	2,147	27.15	1,044	3.89
5,000	10,000	2,884	19,623	1,193	41.37	676	3.45
10,000	20,000	958	12,909	541	56.47	589	4.56
Over	20,000	541	28,826	410	75.79	969	3.36
All		105,218	185,468	12,242	11.63	5,096	2.75

Source: Author's calculations based on estate tax returns filed during 1998-2000; exclude estates with negative wealth.

[a] Wealth is defined as gross estate less debts and estate expenses.
[b] Cumulative lifetime gifts in excess of the annual exclusion, exemption for educational and medical expenses, and gifts to spouse and charities.

Table 12

Determinants of Lifetime Gifts: Choosing Between Gifts and Bequests
(Standard errors reported in parentheses)

Variable	Criterion	Level	Tobit
Constant	-11.0810	-0.4046	-0.8070
	(1.3084)	(0.4538)	(0.1254)
ln Wealth	0.4157	0.0094	0.0262
	(0.0379)	(0.0151)	(0.0033)
Male	-0.1806	--	-0.0217
	(0.0678)	--	(0.0058)
Married	-0.2167	-0.0391	-0.0255
	(0.0725)	(0.0122)	(0.0061)
Number of Children	0.0337	0.0008	0.0027
	(0.0225)	(0.0026)	(0.0021)
Age	0.1108	0.0057	0.0088
	(0.0296)	(0.0050)	(0.0028)
$Age^2 \cdot 10^{-3}$	-0.6906	-0.0314	-0.0523
	(0.1999)	(0.0322)	(0.0187)
Business Share	0.0892	0.0207	0.0182
	(0.1237)	(0.0127)	(0.0116)
ln Gift Tax Price Relative to	-1.1562	-0.1671	-0.1493
Price of Bequests	(0.3752)	(0.0600)	(0.0338)
λ	--	0.0590	--
	--	(0.0536)	--
σ	--	--	0.0993
	--	--	(0.0012)
$\Phi(z)$	0.3709		0.3201
Log-Likelihood	-1,377	1,039	6,923
Observations	2,361	928	2,361

Source: Joulfaian, David. "Choosing Between Gifts and Bequests: How Taxes Affect the Timing of Wealth Transfers," Journal of Public Economics 89:11-12, December, 2005, 2069-2091.

Table 13

Determinants of Lifetime Transfers (1933-1998)
Dependent Variable = ln Gifts$_t$ - ln Gifts$_{t-1}$

Variables	(1)		(2)	
	Coefficient	s.e.	Coefficient	s.e.
Constant	0.0373	0.0741	0.0354	0.0759
d ln Gift Tax Price, lagged	-2.2655	1.5242	-2.2092	1.5833
d ln Gift Tax Price	-14.3710	2.9029	-14.4806	3.0196
d ln Expected Gift Tax Price	13.1663	2.5978	13.4291	3.1577
d ln Expected Bequest Price	--	--	-0.2568	1.7204
d Dummy 1989	0.7267	0.2954	0.7270	0.2981
d ln Real S&P Index	0.2460	0.3796	0.2398	0.3853
d ln Real GDP	0.4365	1.4101	0.5123	1.5108
d ln Real Estate Tax Revenues	0.1170	0.4018	0.1326	0.4186
d ln Real Exemption	-0.4514	0.3430	-0.4290	0.3772
Adjusted R^2	0.4775		0.4681	
Observations	64		64	

Source: Joulfaian, David. "Gift Taxes and Lifetime Transfers: Time Series Evidence," Journal of Public Economics, 88:9-10, August, 2004, 1917-1929.

Table 14

Estimates of Gift Giving Behavior
(Gifts made during 1936-1992 reported by the estates of decedents in 1992)
(Standard errors in parentheses)

Variable	Probability of Making Gifts$_t$	ln Gifts$_t$	Gifts$_t$/ Lifetime Gifts
Intercept	10.89	10.29	6.27
	(1.42)	(1.70)	(2.69)
ln gift tax price	-23.31	-8.38	-27.70
	(3.62)	(4.32)	(6.21)
ln expected gift tax price	17.78	8.45	30.17
	(3.26)	(3.89)	(6.47)
Time	-0.38	0.01	-0.27
	(0.07)	(0.08)	(0.09)
Time^2/100	0.46	0.05	0.28
	(0.04)	(0.05)	(0.07)
Dummy Year 1989	1.77	0.66	5.88
	(0.62)	(0.74)	(1.24)
ln S&P Index	-0.39	0.49	--
	(0.35)	(0.41)	--
Adjusted R^2	0.96	0.82	0.75
Observations	56	56	56

Source: Joulfaian, David and Kathleen McGarry. "Estate and Gift Tax Incentives and Inter Vivos Giving," National Tax Journal, 57:2, Part 2, June 2004.

Table 15

Gifts Reported in Survey Data and on Tax Returns

Gross Gifts per Individual Donor ($000's)			HRS and AHEAD 1992/3 Data			1993 Gift tax Returns		
			Taxable Gifts*			Taxable Gifts*		
			Donors	$millions	Mean	Donors	$millions	Mean
Under		200	372,581	6,517	17,492	110,210	4,773	43,308
200	to	600	-	-	-	22,392	6,791	303,278
600	to	1,000	-	-	-	4,730	2,898	612,685
1,000	to	2,500	-	-	-	880	1,150	1,306,818
2,500	to	5,000	-	-	-	128	423	3,304,688
5,000	to	10,000	-	-	-	54	374	6,925,926
10,000	to	20,000	-	-	-	22	305	13,863,636
20,000	to	30,000	-	-	-	9	212	23,555,556
30,000	over		-	-	-	8	394	49,250,000
Total			372,581	6,517	17,492	138,433	17,319	125,107
Taxable and non-Taxable Gifts**			Donors	$millions	Mean	Donors	$millions	Mean
			15,036,541	45,797	3,046	208,307	23,872	114,600

* Taxable donors and gifts refer to gifts in excess of $10,000 per donee. These become truly taxable when they exceed $600,000. Gifts by married households in HRS and AHEAD are split equally between the spouses. Gifts reported in HRS/AHEAD are not reduced by transfers for educational and medical expenses. Gifts reported on tax returns are not grossed up for the gift tax.

** Include gifts under the annual exclusion of $10,000 ($20,000 for couples).

Figure 1. Gift Tax Receipts: Fiscal Years 1925-2005
($billions)

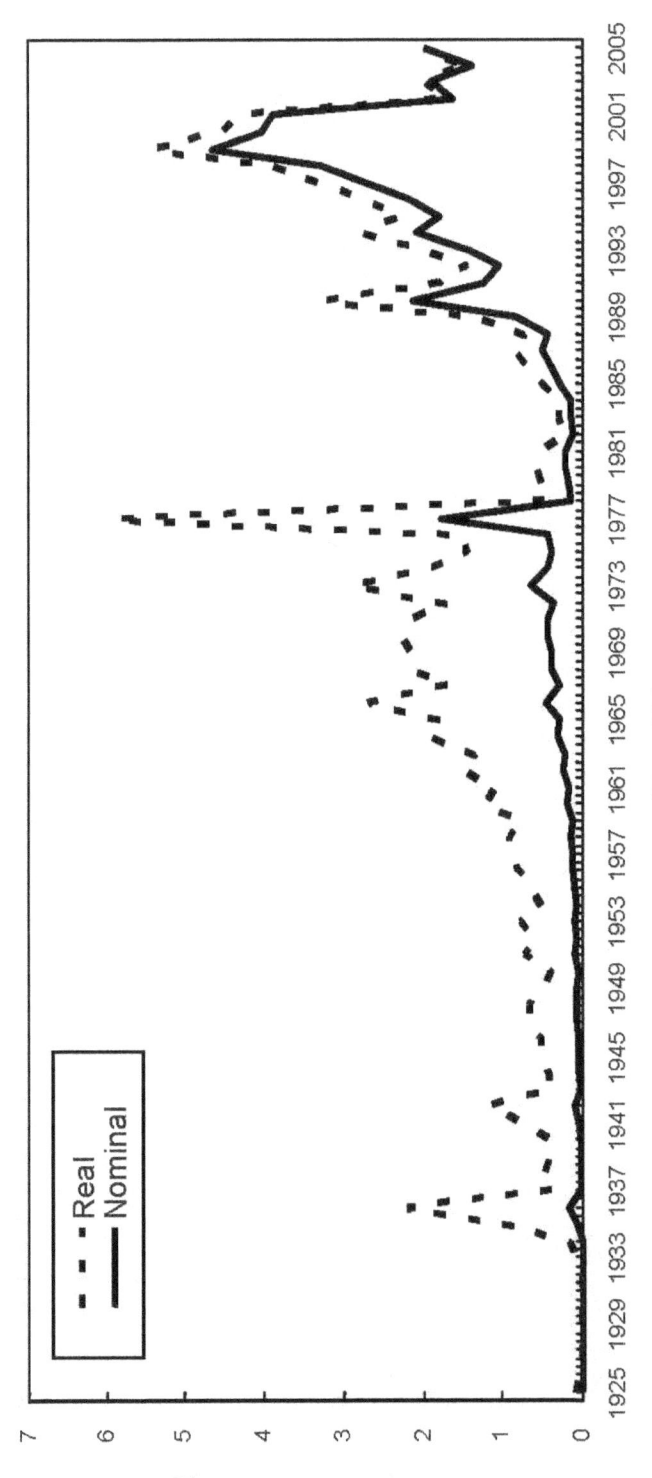

54

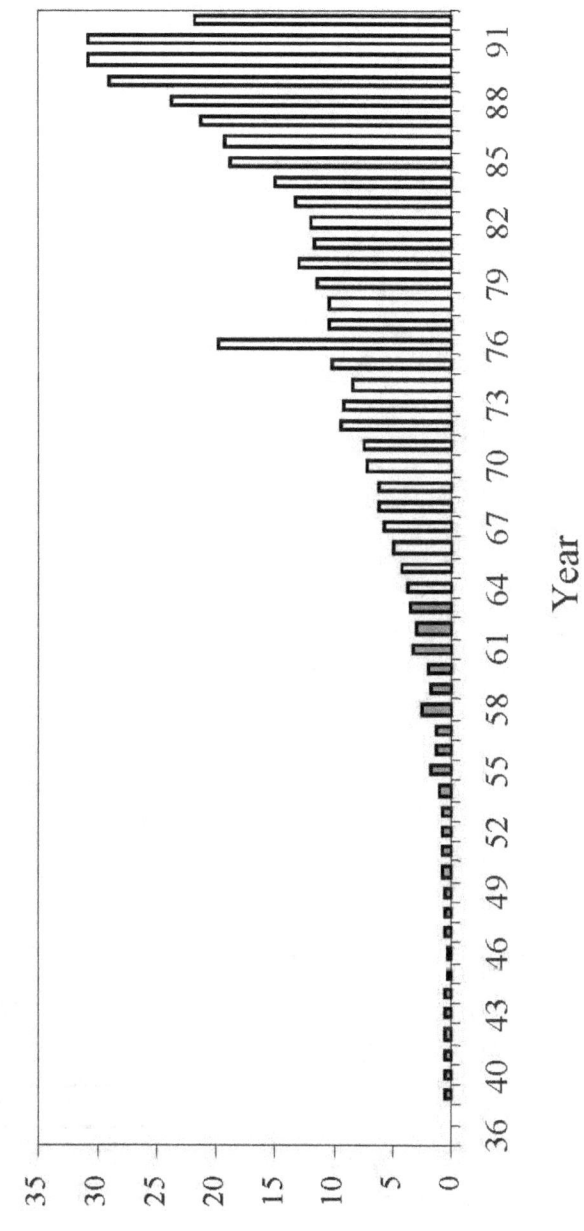

Figure 2. Relative Frequency of Giving by Year

55

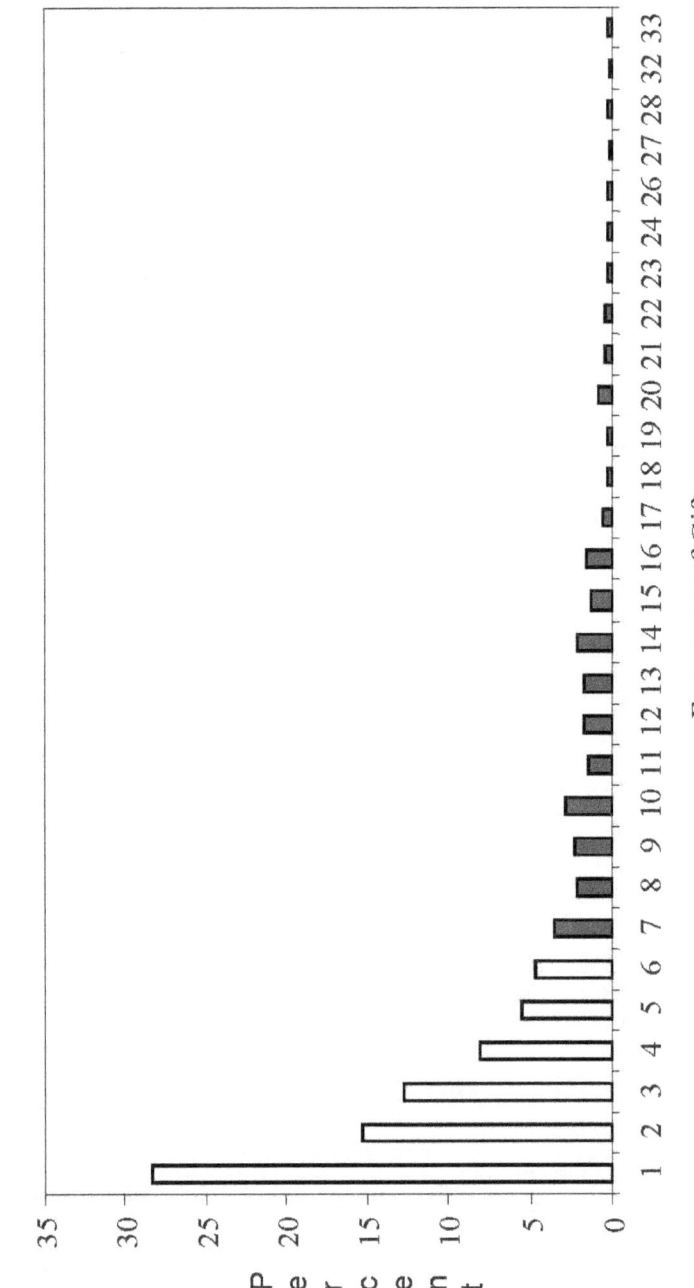

Figure 3. Relative Frequency of Lifetime Gifts

56